journey to the manger

ADVENT CALENDAR

Journey to the Manger Advent Calendar

© 2014, 2015 Focus on the Family

Originally appeared in *Thriving Family Magazine*, December 2014

A Focus on the Family resource published by Tyndale House Publishers, Inc., Carol Stream, Illinois 60188

Illustrations by Luke Flowers

Parents' Guide by Sheila Siefert

Edited by Thriving Family editorial team

Puzzles created by Cary Bates, Jody Reiner, Stephen O'Rear and Sheila Seifert

Designed by Cary Bates and Jody Reiner

Cover design by Mark Anthony Lane II

ISBN: 978-1-58997-824-9

For manufacturing information regarding this product, please call 1-800-323-9400.

Printed in China

21   20

7   6   5   4

How to Use This Guide

As the Advent season unfolds, we hope your family is led on a faith-filled journey to the manger. This book is packed full of devotions, prayers, Scripture and fun activities that will help you guide your children in understanding what the holiday season is truly about.

This book contains an activity, Scripture reading, short lesson and prayer to use each day, along with puzzles and trivia questions to engage the whole family. Some of the daily activities may require some minor advance preparation, so you may want to look ahead to be sure you have all the supplies you will need.

Before you get started, remove the Advent poster and hang it in a central location in your home. Here is how to use this guide:

1. Lead your family in the daily activity, Scripture reading, short lesson and prayer located in the Parents' Guide section.

2. Remove the character of the day sticker and attach to the poster in the correct location.

3. Work on the related puzzle located in the kids' puzzle section of the book.

4. Go online together to either ClubhouseMagazine.com or ClubhouseJr.com to read a related story or article.

Day 1: God the Father

Poster

Have children attach the image of **God the Father** to the Advent poster.

Scripture

Your way, O God, is holy. What god is great like our God? You are the God who works wonders; you have made known your might among the peoples. You with your arm redeemed your people, the children of Jacob and Joseph. *Selah.* (Psalm 77:13-15)

For younger children: Have children say, "He came up with a plan," whenever you point to them. Point to them after each bolded word.

For older children: Ask your children: "What plan might we decide on if all the food in our refrigerator were suddenly moldy? What plan might we have if all our shoes were missing and there were three feet of snow outside? Why are plans important?"

Read: Today begins the first day of Advent. Do you know what Advent is? It is a time of waiting and preparing for the celebration of Christ's birth. It's also a time of remembering why Jesus came as a baby. The Christmas story doesn't start with Jesus' birth. It starts with **God the Father** giving humankind hope. **God** made a perfect world. Then Adam and Eve sinned. Their sin kept them from being near **God**. But the Father loved humankind so much that He came up with a plan to draw all people back to **Him**. **He** came up with a plan even without an apology from Adam and Eve. Over time, God revealed His plan to Hebrew leaders and prophets. What was His plan? **He** was going to send His only Son to live among humans—as a human—and redeem us by taking the punishment for our sins.

Prayer: Ask God for help to forgive others, even without an apology.

Kids' puzzle: Let kids go deeper by reading today's lesson in their booklet, doing the puzzle and exploring related material at **ClubhouseMagazine.com** and **ClubhouseJr.com**.

Day 2: King David

Poster

Have children attach the **King David** image to the Advent poster.

Scripture

And when he [God] had removed him [King Saul], he raised up David to be their king, of whom he testified and said, "I have found in David the son of Jesse a man after my heart, who will do all my will." Of this man's offspring God has brought to Israel a Savior, Jesus, as he promised. (Acts 13:22-23)

For younger children: Have children say, "God forgives mistakes," whenever you point to them. Point to them after each bolded word.

For older children: Tear a cotton ball in half. Wrap a rubber band around it a few times. On one hand, wrap a second rubber band once around your middle finger and your thumb to create a slingshot. Place the rubber-banded cotton ball against the side closest to you and pull back the rubber band. When you let go, the cotton ball will shoot forward. Though not the same sling that David used to kill Goliath, it gives kids the feel for slinging an object. Talk about what David may have used his sling to hit. Then ask children to try to hit a chair with their cotton ball. Count the number of misses and rejoice over any direct hits.

Read: David was a **shepherd** and the **youngest** son of Jesse. **He** didn't possess any worldly importance to make others notice him, but he did have faith in God. After using his sling to kill a giant who wanted to enslave his nation, **David** became a great **warrior** and then a **king**. But **he** also made some big mistakes along the way. Fortunately, each time **he** did, **he** turned back to God and asked for forgiveness. **David's** humble beginnings and his mistakes didn't stop God from using **him**. God said that **David** was a **man** after His own heart. God gave **David** an important role in His plan to redeem the world. **David** became the great-grandfather of Jesus. **David** wasn't perfect, but **he** lived his life for God, and God honored **him**.

Prayer: Ask God to help you be real with each other. Ask God to help you be humble and willing to ask for forgiveness.

Kids' puzzle: Let kids go deeper by reading today's lesson in their booklet, doing the puzzle and exploring related material at **ClubhouseJr.com**.

Day 3: Isaiah

Poster

Have children attach the **Isaiah** image to the Advent poster.

Scripture

Therefore the Lord himself will give you a sign. Behold, the virgin shall conceive and bear a son, and shall call his name Immanuel. (Isaiah 7:14)

For younger children: Have children say, "Don't be scared; God can help!" whenever you point to them. Point to them after each bolded word or phrase.

For older children: Give each family member a sheet of paper. Set a timer for three minutes. Ask everyone to write or draw as many real-world scary things as he or she can. After three minutes, tack all your sheets on the wall. Circle the top three to five scary items that your family has in common. Then pray for God to help you through scary events and rely on Him for hope.

Read: Isaiah lived during **scary times**. People around him were **afraid of enemy armies** that wanted to destroy them. Even the king was **scared**. People didn't want other nations to attack them and **take their things** or hurt their **children**. God didn't want His people to live in **fear**. He wanted them to trust Him, so He told Isaiah to give them an important **message** that would give hope during **scary times**. Isaiah told God's people that someday a baby would be **born**. This baby would save **everyone**, and His name would be Immanuel—*God with us*. Through **Isaiah**, God let His people know that He had not abandoned **them**. He loved them so much that He was willing to leave heaven to save **them**.

Prayer: Ask God to remove the fears of each of your family members this Christmas season and help each of you to turn to Him with your worries.

Kids' puzzle: Let kids go deeper by reading today's lesson in their booklet, doing the puzzle and exploring related material at **ClubhouseMagazine.com**.

Day 4: Micah

Poster

Have children attach the **Micah** image to the Advent poster.

Scripture

But you, O Bethlehem Ephrathah, who are too little to be among the clans of Judah, from you shall come forth for me one who is to be ruler in Israel, whose coming forth is from of old, from ancient days. (Micah 5:2)

For younger children: Have children say, "But that's not fair!" whenever you point to them. Point to them after each bolded word.

For older children: Ask children to tell about something unfair that happened to them recently. Then say: "Why aren't unfair things always made fair? Does God promise to make everything fair? Does He promise to be with you through unfair and hard times? Describe a hard time when you felt God's presence with you as you walked through it."

Read: Micah lived during a time when his country was about to be taken over by another **country**. These were dangerous **times**. He kept telling Israel to stop being unjust and tell God they were sorry. As it happens, they had forgotten to help the **poor**, **widows** and **orphans**. People were unfair in their business deals, and there were people who robbed **others**. Women and children were not treated well, and those who should have been helping these people were instead using the money to buy expensive things for **themselves** and live a life of **ease**. So Micah told them to repent and do what was just. But he also gave them hope. He told them that God would restore Israel someday, and he told them that the Messiah, their Savior, would be born in Bethlehem.

Prayer: Ask God for the ability to seek and recognize His presence during unfair or difficult circumstances.

Kids' puzzle: Let kids go deeper by reading today's lesson in their booklet, doing the puzzle and exploring related material at **ClubhouseMagazine.com**.

Day 5: Zechariah (the prophet)

Poster

Have children attach the **Zechariah (the prophet)** image to the Advent poster.

Scripture

Rejoice greatly, O daughter of Zion! Shout aloud, O daughter of Jerusalem! Behold, your king is coming to you; righteous and having salvation is he, humble and mounted on a donkey, on a colt, the foal of a donkey. (Zechariah 9:9)

For younger children: Have children say, "Is Jesus here yet?" whenever you point to them. Point to them after each bolded word.

For older children: Help your kids make a basket out of wet toilet paper: Give each child a small bowl, plastic wrap and a roll of toilet paper. Have them turn the bowl upside down so the mouth rests on a flat surface. Then cover the outside of the bowl with one layer of plastic wrap. Ask children to wrap several layers of toilet paper around the outside of the bowl. Then have them wet the paper by dipping their hands in water and drenching the toilet paper. Repeat this a number of times until the bowl has a 1/4-inch covering of wet toilet paper around the outside and bottom. Let the toilet paper dry. (Note: This craft will be used as an angel's gown on Day 20, so use a bowl that best reflects that shape, and save this craft when you have finished it.) Talk about how it might take a day or more for their toilet-paper bowl to dry. Why might you get discouraged if you had to wait a full year or five years for your basket to dry?

Read: Zechariah might have been a fun prophet to **know**. He told God's people to **repent**, but he also encouraged them with words of hope. He told them that God was faithful and would remember all of His promises. One of God's promises was that He'd send a **Savior**, His **Son**, so the Hebrew people could draw near to **God** again. God's people needed this hope because it would be a **long time** before the Messiah would come. Zechariah had no idea how many **days, years** . . . even *centuries* his people would have to **wait**. But he did know that God would someday send a Savior.

Prayer: Ask God to give His hope to each of your family members this Christmas season.

Kids' puzzle: Let kids go deeper by reading today's lesson in their booklet, doing the puzzle and exploring related material at **ClubhouseMagazine.com.**

Day 6: Anna

Poster

Have children attach the **Anna** image to the Advent poster.

Scripture

And there was a prophetess, Anna, the daughter of Phanuel, of the tribe of Asher. She was advanced in years, having lived with her husband seven years from when she was a virgin, and then as a widow until she was eighty-four. She did not depart from the temple, worshiping with fasting and prayer night and day. And coming up at that very hour she began to give thanks to God and to speak of him to all who were waiting for the redemption of Jerusalem. (Luke 2:36-38)

For younger children: Have children say, "Pay attention to God!" whenever you point to them. Point to them after each bolded word.

For older children: Gather 25 small items from your home and place them on a tray. Keep the items displayed for one minute, and then cover them with a cloth. Have your kids work together to list all 25 items. When you're done, talk about the difference between noticing things on your own and working with others to remember things.

Read: Anna was an old **woman**. She had spent most of her life living at the **temple**. She prayed at the **temple**. She worshiped at the **temple**. But she didn't know who would someday be coming to the **temple**. She didn't stay at the temple because she had to but because she *wanted* to. She enjoyed **talking** to God and **praising** Him. She didn't seem to want to **miss** a moment of honoring Him with her life. Then God gave her a wonderful gift. When Mary and Joseph came with their child, she was able to recognize Jesus as the Savior. As Jesus was presented at the **temple** 40 days after He was **born**, Anna was there to see, hear and celebrate Jesus' **birth**.

Prayer: Ask God to help your family pay attention to what He wants to do in your lives.

Kids' puzzle: Let kids go deeper by reading today's lesson in their booklet, doing the puzzle and exploring related material at **ClubhouseMagazine.com.**

Day 7: Simeon

Poster

Have children attach the **Simeon** image to the Advent poster.

Scripture

Now there was a man in Jerusalem, whose name was Simeon, and this man was righteous and devout, waiting for the consolation of Israel, and the Holy Spirit was upon him. And it had been revealed to him by the Holy Spirit that he would not see death before he had seen the Lord's Christ. (Luke 2:25-26)

For younger children: Have children say, "God promised," whenever you point to them. Point to them after each bolded word.

For older children: Place a small wastebasket on the floor. From the other side of the room, have children toss crumpled paper toward the target. Talk about how frustrating it can be to miss the wastebasket. Talk about how life's circumstances can be frustrating and feel nearly impossible to overcome. Then gradually shorten the distance between them and the wastebasket, to see how many baskets they can make.

Read: God told Simeon that he wouldn't die until he'd seen the **Messiah**. So Simeon waited and **waited** and grew older and **older**. Some people may have become discouraged by the long **wait**, but Simeon **didn't**. Then one day, God's Spirit led Simeon to the temple. He probably didn't know why he had to go to the temple that day. It may have been inconvenient for him. He may have had other plans. Still, Simeon went to the temple and met His **Savior**. Sometimes it's the little things we do, the things that are not in our plans or that are inconvenient, that give us the most **joy** in the long run. Simeon saw Jesus and recognized Him as the Messiah. God kept His promise to Simeon.

Prayer: Ask God to help you follow the Spirit's leading so you won't miss out on the plans that He has for you.

Kids' puzzle: Let kids go deeper by reading today's lesson in their booklet, doing the puzzle and exploring related material at **ClubhouseJr.com**.

Day 8: Angel Gabriel

Poster

Have children attach the **angel Gabriel** image to the Advent poster.

Scripture

In the sixth month the angel Gabriel was sent from God to a city of Galilee named Nazareth, to a virgin betrothed to a man whose name was Joseph, of the house of David. And the virgin's name was Mary. . . . And the angel said to her, "Do not be afraid, Mary, for you have found favor with God. And behold, you will conceive in your womb and bear a son, and you shall call his name Jesus." (Luke 1:26-27, 30-31)

For younger children: Have children say, "God has a message!" whenever you point to them. Point to them after each bolded word.

For older children: Discuss these questions with your kids: "What would you do if an angel came to your house or your school? How would you act? What would you say? Do you think most people would be afraid if Gabriel came and spoke to them, or would they warmly welcome him? How would you treat Gabriel if he visited you?"

Read: The angel **Gabriel** had a message from God for a man named Zechariah, who was a priest. **Gabriel** went to the man's workplace, which was the temple. **Gabriel** told Zechariah that something impossible was going to happen: He and his wife would have a son. **Gabriel's** words were hard to believe because Zechariah and his wife were now too old to have children. **Gabriel** said their son would tell others about Jesus' coming. **Gabriel** not only got to tell Zechariah that he and his wife would have a miracle baby, but he also got to tell a young woman named Mary that she would be the mother of the Christ. He told Mary of the Messiah's coming greatness, how He would sit on the throne of King David and be the ruler from that day forward. **Gabriel** knew that nothing was impossible for God. He was the right messenger for this Good **News** that was of great joy to many!

Prayer: Ask God to help your family be the bearer of the Good News to a hurting world.

Kids' puzzle: Let kids go deeper by reading today's lesson in their booklet, doing the puzzle and exploring related material at **ClubhouseJr.com**.

And there appeared to him an angel of the Lord standing on the right side of the altar of incense. And Zechariah was troubled when he saw him, and fear fell upon him. But the angel said to him, "Do not be afraid, Zechariah, for your prayer has been heard, and your wife Elizabeth will bear you a son, and you shall call his name John." (Luke 1:11-13)

Have children attach the **Elizabeth** image to the Advent poster.

In those days Mary arose and went with haste into the hill country, to a town in Judah, and she entered the house of Zechariah and greeted Elizabeth. And when Elizabeth heard the greeting of Mary, the baby leaped in her womb. And Elizabeth was filled with the Holy Spirit, and she exclaimed with a loud cry, "Blessed are you among women, and blessed is the fruit of your womb! And why is this granted to me that the mother of my Lord should come to me? For behold, when the sound of your greeting came to my ears, the baby in my womb leaped for joy. And blessed is she who believed that there would be a fulfillment of what was spoken to her from the Lord." (Luke 1:39-45)

Day 9: Zechariah (John's father)

For younger children: Have children cover their mouths and try to say, "He can't talk," whenever you point to them. Point to them after each bolded word.

For older children: Hide a treat or a prize somewhere in the room and let your children see you hide it. Explain that all they have to do is tell you where it is to get it. The problem is that they can't use any words or sounds, and they can't get it themselves. Sit down, and let them find a way to lead you to the prize. Act as if you don't know what they want, so that even if they point to it, say things like, "You look like you're dancing," and then mimic their actions. Through this activity, help them see how challenging life can be when they can no longer use their voice.

Read: Zechariah didn't lose his voice because of a cold or the flu, but he was unable to talk for **months** and **months**. Remember the angel Gabriel from yesterday? Gabriel came to Zechariah after Zechariah was chosen to enter the sanctuary of the temple in Jerusalem. Gabriel told Zechariah that his wife would have a baby, but Zechariah didn't believe him. So Gabriel stopped Zechariah from being able to speak until the baby was **born**. Have you guessed Zechariah's relationship to the baby Jesus (who wasn't yet born)? He would be the father of Jesus' cousin John the Baptist. God the Father was preparing for Jesus' birth and life on earth. Zechariah becoming a father was one of these **preparations**. God wanted Zechariah's child to **tell** people that Jesus was coming.

Prayer: Ask God to help your family use their words to please God and say what He wants them to say.

Kids' puzzle: Let kids go deeper by reading today's lesson in their booklet, doing the puzzle and exploring related material at **ClubhouseMagazine.com**.

Day 10: Elizabeth

For younger children: Have children say about Mary, "Blessed are you among women!" whenever you point to them. Point to them after each bolded word.

For older children: Often we will greet people in different ways. Have one person in your family act like each of these people: stranger, someone asking for directions, someone you don't know well in class, a friend, a best friend, sibling, parent, aunt/uncle, grandparent, storekeeper, librarian, police officer, president of the United States. Have others in the family practice greeting these "people" according to how well you know the person or how much honor you give the person.

Read: Elizabeth was Zechariah's wife, and she became pregnant when she was past the age of being able to have children. How her life must have changed! Her husband couldn't speak while she was pregnant, and she had to prepare for a new baby. When Mary, a cousin, visited, Elizabeth recognized that **God** had come to earth as a **child**. She said to Mary, "Blessed are you among **women**, and blessed is the fruit of your **womb**!" Jesus was really, really **small** and not yet **born**, but Elizabeth greeted her cousin Mary with **words** that came from the Holy Spirit.

Prayer: Ask God to help your family celebrate Jesus every day.

Kids' puzzle: Let kids go deeper by reading today's lesson in their booklet, doing the puzzle and exploring related material at **ClubhouseJr.com**.

Day 11: John the Baptist

Poster

Have children attach the **John the Baptist** image to the Advent poster.

Scripture

But the angel said to him, "Do not be afraid, Zechariah, for your prayer has been heard, and your wife Elizabeth will bear you a son, and you shall call his name John." (Luke 1:13)

For younger children: Have children say, "Get ready for Jesus!" whenever you point to them. Point to them after each bolded word.

For older children: Discuss these questions with your kids: "When it's time to go somewhere—church, the grocery store or school—what are all the steps included in our 'getting ready'? What happens if we don't get ready at the right time? What might happen if we didn't get ready in the correct way, such as putting our shoes on our hands or dressing inappropriately for the weather?"

Read: John the Baptist was given a big task. He had to tell people to get ready for the Messiah. God helped introduce the **world** to His Son, Jesus, through John, who was an earthly **cousin**. God knew that John was special, and He had an angel tell John's **father**, Zechariah, that his son would play an important role in Jesus' life. He would be filled with the Holy Spirit from an early age and his life would be spent preparing people's hearts for **Jesus**.

Prayer: Ask God to help your family serve Him in all you do, so God will be glorified.

Kids' puzzle: Let kids go deeper by reading today's lesson in their booklet, doing the puzzle and exploring related material at **ClubhouseMagazine.com** and **ClubhouseJr.com**.

Day 12: King Herod

Poster

Have children attach the **King Herod** image to the Advent poster.

Scripture

Now after Jesus was born in Bethlehem of Judea in the days of Herod the king, behold, wise men from the east came to Jerusalem, saying, "Where is he who has been born king of the Jews? For we saw his star when it rose and have come to worship him." When Herod the king heard this, he was troubled, and all Jerusalem with him. (Matthew 2:1-3)

For younger children: Have children say, "I want what I want. Waaa!" whenever you point to them. Point to them after each bolded word.

For older children: Discuss these questions with your kids: "Can you tell me about a time when you didn't get your way? What did you have to do instead? How might not getting your way actually make you a more mature person? What happens to people who always get their way? Do you like being around them? Why shouldn't we always get our way?"

Read: **King Herod** did many evil things, and **he** often acted like a spoiled **child**. He was known as Herod the Great, but he wasn't "great" at **all**. He was mean to others and always tried to get his **way**. He didn't care how he hurt **others**. He told the wise men to go find Jesus, but **he** did not try to find Jesus nor did he want to worship Jesus. Being king was the most important thing to **him**. Yet Jesus—born as King of the Jews and the King of **all** kings—had power over even King **Herod**.

Prayer: Ask God to help your family do what is right by others, even if it means that you don't get what you want.

Kids' puzzle: Let kids go deeper by reading today's lesson in their booklet, doing the puzzle and exploring related material at **ClubhouseMagazine.com**.

Day 13: High Priest

Poster

Have children attach the **high priest** image to the Advent poster.

For younger children: Have children say, "Love and obey your God" whenever you point to them. Point to them after each bolded word or phrase.

For older children: Have one child make a map to something he or she has hidden. Ask the rest of the family to find that object using the map. If part of the map is confusing, have family members ask the child to clarify. The child can help interpret the picture until the objects are found.

Read: In the Jewish tradition, **high priests** were meant to show people the way to **God**. The **high priest** was supposed to be someone who loved God, followed His instructions and demonstrated His love to **others**. But the **role** became a job that people abused, leading them to become powerful and prideful. They ordered people around as a king would. By the time Jesus was born, the high priest was no longer a **position** that served others. But by the time Jesus' work on earth was done, there was no longer a need for a human high priest. Jesus filled that position as our great **High Priest**.

Prayer: Ask God to help you show others how to love Him.

Kids' puzzle: Let kids go deeper by reading today's lesson in their booklet, doing the puzzle and exploring related material at **ClubhouseJr.com**.

Scripture

For every high priest chosen from among men is appointed to act on behalf of men in relation to God, to offer gifts and sacrifices for sins. . . . So also Christ did not exalt himself to be made a high priest, but was appointed by him who said to him, "You are my Son, today I have begotten you." (Hebrews 5:1, 5)

Day 14: Caesar Augustus

Poster

Have children attach the **Caesar Augustus** image to the Advent poster.

For younger children: Have children say, "How many people do I rule?" whenever you point to them. Point to them after each bolded word.

For older children: Have each person create an imaginary census. Explain that a census is a record of who people are and where they live. Read the following line and have each child fill in the blanks: "A decree went out from [your first name] to the whole [last name] family and told everyone to register all the [what is being counted] in the house." Then the family should count the chairs or dogs or jelly beans or whatever is mentioned for the census. When one census is complete, have the next child conduct another census for you.

Read: A **decree** went out from Caesar Augustus to the whole Roman **world** that told all people to **register** in their hometown. Caesar wanted to know how many **people** he ruled. So all of the people had to stop what they were doing, travel to their hometown and be counted in the **census**. This **census** required that Mary and Joseph travel to Bethlehem, which helped fulfill Micah's prophecy that the Messiah would be born in **Bethlehem**. So God used Caesar Augustus—**someone** who didn't believe in Him—to cause His will to be done.

Prayer: Thank God for using even unbelievers to accomplish His will.

Kids' puzzle: Let kids go deeper by reading today's lesson in their booklet, doing the puzzle and exploring related material at **ClubhouseJr.com**.

Scripture

In those days a decree went out from Caesar Augustus that all the world should be registered. This was the first registration when Quirinius was governor of Syria. And all went to be registered, each to his own town. (Luke 2:1-3)

Day 15: Donkey

For younger children: Have children say, "Hee-haw, hee-haw," whenever you point to them. Point to them after each bolded word.

For older children: Play a game of pin the tail on the donkey. Talk about the characteristics of donkeys and how God may have used this animal while Jesus was on earth.

Read: **Donkeys** were common animals during New Testament times. **They** were used for carrying cargo or other heavy loads. When Jesus came into the world, He was laid in a manger, the food bin for a **donkey** or another animal. Mary may have ridden a donkey when she entered Bethlehem. If a donkey was present at Jesus' birth, the animal would have been a reminder of Jesus' humble beginnings, but these creatures also played a special part in Jesus' story during His life on earth. As a grown man, Jesus rode on a **donkey** on His final visit into Jerusalem to declare Himself the Prince of Peace.

Prayer: Pray for the ability to remain humble with whatever work God gives your family, so you can glorify Him.

Kids' puzzle: Let kids go deeper by reading today's lesson in their booklet, doing the puzzle and exploring related material at **ClubhouseMagazine.com** and **ClubhouseJr.com**.

Poster

Have children attach the **donkey** image to the Advent poster.

Scripture

"Fear not, daughter of Zion; behold, your king is coming, sitting on a donkey's colt!" (John 12:15)

Day 16: Innkeeper

For younger children: Have children say, "No room," whenever you point to them. Point to them after each bolded word.

For older children: Discuss these questions with your kids: "What is your bedtime ritual—food, drink, covers, time for bed? How does this ritual help you sleep? When you need a good night's sleep, do you like to change your bedtime ritual? Why might the innkeeper have not wanted to give up his bed to Mary and Joseph? If you gave up your bed to someone, where would you sleep? How would that affect your sleep?"

Read: Was there an innkeeper who turned Mary and Joseph away from an **inn**? We don't know. What we do know is that there was "no place for them in the inn," and **someone**—perhaps a relative or perhaps a stranger—offered them a place to spend the night where animals usually **stayed**. Because of this, we know that Jesus was born in a humble place that wasn't set up for the King of heaven and earth. Think about what the full inn caused **someone** to miss out on. This **person** got to sleep in her own inn and in her own bed, exchanging one night of comfort for a once-in-all-eternity opportunity to be of physical service to God's Son.

Prayer: Ask God to help your family recognize opportunities to exchange comfort for the chance to bring Him glory.

Kids' puzzle: Let kids go deeper by reading today's lesson in their booklet, doing the puzzle and exploring related material at **ClubhouseJr.com**.

Poster

Have children attach the **innkeeper** image to the Advent poster.

Scripture

And she gave birth to her firstborn son and wrapped him in swaddling cloths and laid him in a manger, because there was no place for them in the inn. (Luke 2:7)

Day 17: Sheep

Poster

Have children attach the **sheep** image to the Advent poster.

Scripture

And in the same region there were shepherds out in the field, keeping watch over their flock by night. (Luke 2:8)

For younger children: Have children say, "Baa! Baa!" whenever you point to them. Point to them after each bolded word.

For older children: Have children shut their eyes, or you can blindfold them. The goal will be for them to move from one side of your house to the other with only your voice guiding them. You should tell them when to take a step, when something is in the way or when to wait while you move something from their path. Then compare this experience to a flock of sheep needing a shepherd.

Read: **Sheep** aren't very smart. **They** eat, **they** bleat, **they** grow wool for people to make into clothing. In some places, sheep are used for food. Sheep must trust that a shepherd will take care of **them**, that he'll protect **them** and guide **them** to safe pastures. Jesus compares many human actions to the actions of **sheep**. Jesus is our Good Shepherd, and He takes care of **us**. Just as sheep recognize the voice of their shepherd, so should we recognize the voice of our Savior. God's announcement of the Messiah's birth came to shepherds who were watching their **sheep** at night, men who understood these simple, helpless **animals**. At this time of year, it's good to remember that we are Jesus' **flock**, to better understand how He cares for us.

Prayer: Ask God to help you hear the voice of your Shepherd and follow Him.

Kids' puzzle: Let kids go deeper by reading today's lesson in their booklet, doing the puzzle and exploring related material at **ClubhouseMagazine.com**.

Day 18: Angel

Poster

Have children attach the **angel** image to the Advent poster.

Scripture

And an angel of the Lord appeared to them, and the glory of the Lord shone around them, and they were filled with great fear. And the angel said to them, "Fear not, for behold, I bring you good news of great joy that will be for all the people. For unto you is born this day in the city of David a Savior, who is Christ the Lord. And this will be a sign for you: you will find a baby wrapped in swaddling cloths and lying in a manger." (Luke 2:9-12)

For younger children: Have children say, "Good news! Good news!" whenever you point to them. Point to them after each bolded word.

For older children: Let your children know that they will be reading today's Advent entry. Sit in a circle. Have someone read two words and pass it to the next person to read the next two words. Then repeat it so everyone reads three words, then four words, and so on until the Advent entry below is read. In this way, everyone has the chance to be the messenger of good news.

Read: **Someone** had to tell the shepherds about Jesus. Soon the sky would be filled with **angels**, and their **praises** would ring throughout the heavens, but the shepherds wouldn't have known why they were **singing** if an **angel** didn't tell them. So one **angel** was chosen and given the honor of telling the shepherds that their Savior was born. How thrilled this **angel** must have been. How excited he must have been to see the shepherds' response. After his words, **he** probably joined in with the angelic chorus, praising God and having a glorious time knowing Jesus was born.

Prayer: Ask God to give you the right words at the right time to tell others about Jesus.

Kids' puzzle: Let kids go deeper by reading today's lesson in their booklet, doing the puzzle and exploring related material at **ClubhouseMagazine.com**.

Day 19: Shepherds

Poster

Have children attach the **shepherds** image to the Advent poster.

Scripture

When the angels went away from them into heaven, the shepherds said to one another, "Let us go over to Bethlehem and see this thing that has happened, which the Lord has made known to us." And they went with haste and found Mary and Joseph, and the baby lying in a manger. (Luke 2:15-16)

For younger children: Have children say, "But they're nobody," whenever you point to them. Point to them after each bolded word.

For older children: Camping is fun, but you can get quite dirty as you camp. Sit in a circle. Say, "I went camping with my family, but I got really messy when I [action]." The action should be a way someone could get dirty, such as falling in the dirt or having the dog shake and spray you with dirty water. The second person should repeat what the first person said and add another way to get dirty while camping. The whole family can prompt each other. The goal is to reach 12 ways to become dirty to better understand how filthy the shepherds who came to see Jesus might have been. Shepherds watched their sheep for long periods of time, camping with the flock.

Read: **Shepherds** certainly weren't rich or powerful during Bible times. **They** were the lowly workers making an honest day's wage. **They** were probably dirty and smelly, and **they** didn't get to hang around people in the city very often. They were looked down on by some because they were **shepherds**. And for **them**, the night of Christ's birth probably began as any other night—just another night of watching and protecting sheep—until an angel told the **shepherds** to go and see the Christ child. And the sky filled with angels and music. **They**, the lowest of the **low**, were invited to celebrate the Messiah's birth. In that moment, God demonstrated that it didn't matter who you were or what the world thought of you. Christ came for everyone! So the **shepherds** heard the announcement of His Son's birth, and **they** hurried to welcome the Christ child. Once they saw Him, they went and told others about Him. The fact that they were lowly **shepherds** didn't stop them from sharing the Good News!

Prayer: Ask God to help you see others as God sees them.

Kids' puzzle: Let kids go deeper by reading today's lesson in their booklet, doing the puzzle and exploring related material at **ClubhouseJr.com**.

Day 20: Heavenly Host

Poster

Have children attach the **heavenly host** image to the Advent poster.

Scripture

And suddenly there was with the angel a multitude of the heavenly host praising God and saying, "Glory to God in the highest, and on earth peace among those with whom he is pleased!" (Luke 2:13-14)

For younger children: Have children ask, "Do you see Him?" whenever you point to them. Point to them after each bolded word.

For older children: Turn over the basket you made on day five and use it as an angel's gown. Glue on a paper or Styrofoam head and paper or chenille stems (pipe cleaners) as wings. Decorate the gown as you talk about all the songs the angels may have sung to praise Jesus.

Read: Imagine how the angels **felt**. Since the fall of Adam and Eve, all of heaven and earth had been **waiting** for the coming **Messiah**. The angels **watched** and **waited** for the moment when God would save humankind and draw them into relationship with Him. The **angels** were probably very excited, filling the sky with their praises of God's glory. What an honor **they** must have felt as they welcomed the Savior with their songs.

Prayer: Praise God for all His miraculous ways and glorious deeds.

Kids' puzzle: Let kids go deeper by reading today's lesson in their booklet, doing the puzzle and exploring related material at **ClubhouseJr.com**.

Day 21: Wise Men on a Journey

Poster

Have children attach the **wise man on camel** image to the Advent poster.

Scripture

Now after Jesus was born in Bethlehem of Judea in the days of Herod the king, behold, wise men from the east came to Jerusalem. (Matthew 2:1)

For younger children: Have children say, "Let's get going," whenever you point to them. Point to them after each bolded word.

For older children: Ask kids what God put in the sky as a sign to Noah that He would never destroy the earth by water again. "How might nonbelievers view the rainbow? What sign did God put in the sky to tell the world that a great King had been born? How might people at the time have reasoned away that star, if they even noticed it?"

Read: Suddenly a star appeared in the **East**. Most people just went about their daily lives, but a few wise men who studied the stars knew what the appearance of this star **meant**. It meant that a new King had been **born**. They didn't know **where**, and they didn't know how long it would take them to find this new **King**, but they started on a **journey** to find the new King and honorably welcome Him. Through the appearance of a star, the heavens glorified Jesus at His **birth**. And when this **event** happened, it allowed those who lived far from Bethlehem to rejoice that the King had been **born**.

Prayer: Thank God for revealing His Son to you, so that you can believe in Him and receive new life.

Kids' puzzle: Let kids go deeper by reading today's lesson in their booklet, doing the puzzle and exploring related material at **ClubhouseJr.com**.

Day 22: Wise Men Talk with Herod

Poster

Have children attach the **wise man with Herod** image to the Advent poster.

Scripture

"In Bethlehem of Judea, for so it is written by the prophet: 'And you, O Bethlehem, in the land of Judah, are by no means least among the rulers of Judah; for from you shall come a ruler who will shepherd my people Israel.'" (Matthew 2:5-6)

For younger children: Have children say, "Where is the King?" whenever you point to them. Point to them after each bolded word or phrase.

For older children: Help your children create a scroll: First, tape or glue five pieces of printer paper together end to end. Next, roll the scroll on each side to form loops. Then write the prophecy that the scribes quoted (found in today's Scripture verse) on the scroll. Finally, have family members pretend to be the wise men and the scribes from the Advent reading below. Give each child a turn to read the location of the Savior.

Read: The **wise men** traveled far. **They** may have traveled for a few years, or it may have taken some time to prepare for their trip before **they** started. Some scholars think that Jesus may have been almost two years old by the time the wise men arrived in Jerusalem and found their way to King Herod's court. **They** had mistakenly assumed that Herod would know about the new King of the Jews. **They** probably wondered why the new King was not in King Herod's grand palace. But the news of a new King in his kingdom made King Herod angry. He wanted to be the only king of the Jews. Instead of showing his anger, though, Herod pretended to help the **wise men**. He asked his scribes to find the birthplace of the prophesied Messiah. The scribes told the **wise men** that the child would be born in Bethlehem. As the **wise men** hurried on their way, **they** once again saw the star. Although **they** had agreed to tell Herod where **they** found the child, **they** didn't because God had warned them in a dream to return home a different way.

Prayer: Ask God to show your family how to be wise when dealing with people, to discern whether others have good or bad intentions.

Kids' puzzle: Let kids go deeper by reading today's lesson in their booklet, doing the puzzle and exploring related material at **ClubhouseJr.com**.

Day 23: Wise Men Offer Gifts

For younger children: Have children say, "These gifts are for you," whenever yo point to them. Point to them after each bolded word.

For older children: Have each person in the family go into his or her own room and choose one gift to give Jesus. Each person can then present his or her gift and expla why that item would honor the Christ child.

Read: The wise men brought gifts to share with the new **King**. They brought gold, frankincense and myrrh. These gifts were intended for a **king**. During Bible times, simi gifts were given to other **kings**. They were a symbol of **honor** brought from the East. Th Jesus wasn't in a palace and wasn't dressed in costly gowns didn't keep the wise men fro giving Him their **gifts**. Later, when Jesus, Mary and Joseph had to flee Bethlehem becau of King Herod, these valuable and costly **gifts** probably helped them support their smal family while in Egypt.

Prayer: Ask God what gift—your time, your possessions or your talents—you can give Jesus today.

Kids' puzzle: Let kids go deeper by reading today's lesson in their booklet, doing the puzzle and exploring related material at **ClubhouseMagazine.com** and **ClubhouseJr.com**.

Poster

Have children attach the **wise man with gift** image to the Advent poster.

Scripture

When they saw the star, they rejoiced exceedingly with great joy. And going into the house they saw the child with Mary his mother, and they fell down and worshiped him. Then, opening their treasures, they offered him gifts, gold and frankincense and myrrh.
(Matthew 2:10-11)

Day 24: Joseph

For younger children: Have children say, "He took care of Jesus," whenever you point to them. Point to them after each bolded word.

For older children: Show children how to hit a nail with a hammer into a block of wood. Do this in the same way that Joseph might have taught Jesus when teaching th boy carpentry.

Read: **Joseph** was chosen by God to be the **earthly father** of Jesus. **He** was a **carpent** by trade and appeared to have worked at this trade in Nazareth until his death, somewhere between Jesus' 12th and 30th birthdays. Perhaps you wonder why God chos this particular **man**. We don't know for certain, but we can guess that **he** was a **man** wh honored the one true God from deep inside his heart and through his outward actions. Once **he** was told in a dream to take Mary as his wife, **he** traveled with her to Bethleher Being warned in a dream about Herod's plan to kill Jesus, he took his family to Egypt. After Herod's death, he led his family back to Nazareth where **he** probably lived out his days.

Prayer: Ask God how to do His will, whether His will was already a part of your pla for the day or not.

Kids' puzzle: Let kids go deeper by reading today's lesson in their booklet, doing the puzzle and exploring related material at **ClubhouseJr.com**.

Poster

Have children attach the **Joseph** image to the Advent poster.

Scripture

"Joseph, son of David, do not fear to take Mary as your wife, for that which is conceived in her is from the Holy Spirit. She will bear a son, and you shall call his name Jesus, for he will save his people from their sins." (Matthew 1:20-21)

Day 25: Mary

For younger children: Have children say, "Jesus' mother," whenever you point to them. Point to them after each bolded word.

For older children: Ask your children to come up with a job description for a position of their choosing, such as a chef, pastor, president of the United States, etc. Ask them: "What qualifications would the perfect person for the job have? If someone put you in that job right now, would you feel qualified to do it? Would you accept or not accept the job?" Then ask: "What would be in a job description for 'mother of Jesus'?" After they come up with a list, explain that what mattered most to God was her faithfulness and trust in Him. "Do you think Mary felt qualified? Why did she accept the job?"

Read: **Mary** agreed to be the mother of the Messiah and knew that God had honored her. Yet how it worked out wasn't exactly "ideal" according to the custom of the day. **Mary** was young and became pregnant before **she** was married. Then **she** had to travel to another city to be counted in a census shortly before Jesus was born. And at God's appointed time, **Mary** gave birth to the Savior of the world in a stable in Bethlehem. After His birth, Mary had to flee Bethlehem to save her Son's life. **She** lived for a short time in Egypt and then settled in Nazareth, a small town of no consequence. Sometimes things don't turn out like you expect, but **Mary** was willing to trust God and allow Him to show **her** what to do next.

Prayer: Ask for wisdom for each person in your family to trust God with his or her life.

Kids' puzzle: Let kids go deeper by reading today's lesson in their booklet, doing the puzzle and exploring related material at **ClubhouseJr.com**.

Poster

Have children attach the **Mary** image to the Advent poster.

Scripture

"Greetings, O favored one, the Lord is with you!" But she was greatly troubled at the saying, and tried to discern what sort of greeting this might be. And the angel said to her, "Do not be afraid, Mary, for you have found favor with God. And behold, you will conceive in your womb and bear a son, and you shall call his name Jesus." (Luke 1:28-31)

Christmas Day Celebration: Jesus

For older and younger children: Sing "Happy Birthday" to Jesus.

Read: Advent ends on Christmas Eve because Advent is a time of waiting. Christmas Day, on the other hand, is a day of celebration. The waiting is over! It's a time to rejoice at our Savior's birth and to spread the Good News as the angels did many years ago. It's time to honor God with our gifts, as the wise men did, and to hurry to be with Him, as the shepherds did. Merry Christmas!

Prayer: Ask God to show you how to celebrate His Son's birth with all you are and all you have.

Kids' puzzle: Let kids go deeper by reading today's lesson in their booklet, doing the puzzle and exploring related material at **ClubhouseMagazine.com**.

Poster

Have children attach the **Jesus** image to the Advent poster.

Scripture

For God so loved the world, that he gave his only Son, that whoever believes in him should not perish but have eternal life. (John 3:16)

journey
to the manger
KIDS' PUZZLES

More Advent fun inside!

✓ Bible fact

Why did God the Father need a plan to save humankind?
God the Father is holy. That is His nature. Only those who haven't sinned, who are pure in heart, can be near Him. But no one was that pure. Because of sin, the human race could not be near Him.

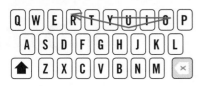

Just for fun

Spell a word on the keyboard to reveal a path. Match that path to the coded pattern below. Put that word on the line below it.

WHAT • WAY • OUR • IS • GOD • LIKE • O • GREAT • ~~YOUR~~ • HOLY

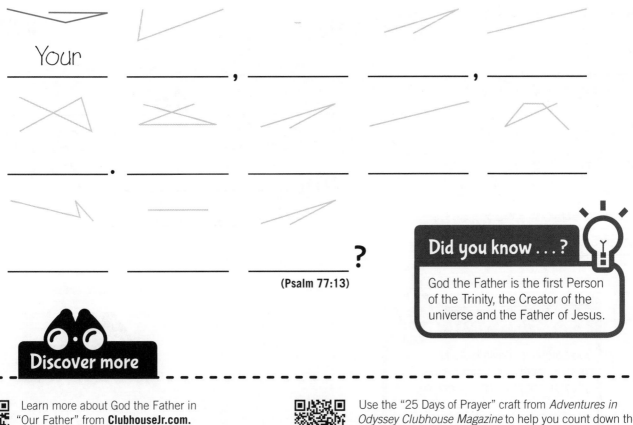

Your

_____ , _____ ,

_____ .

_____ _____ _____ ?

(Psalm 77:13)

💡 Did you know . . . ?

God the Father is the first Person of the Trinity, the Creator of the universe and the Father of Jesus.

👀 Discover more

Learn more about God the Father in "Our Father" from **ClubhouseJr.com.**

ClubhouseJr.com/bible/our-father

Use the "25 Days of Prayer" craft from *Adventures in Odyssey Clubhouse Magazine* to help you count down the days until Christmas.

ClubhouseMagazine.com/create/25-days-of-prayer

DAY 2
King David

Just for fun

Match the rocks from David's pouch with the letters to form part of today's Scripture.

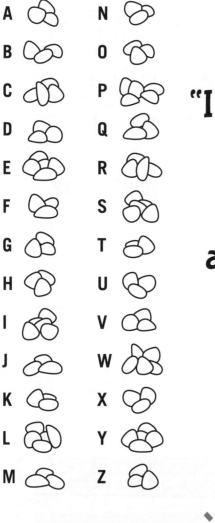

"I have _ _ _ _ _ in David

the son of Jesse a _ _ _

after my _ _ _ _ _ , who

_ _ _ _ _ do _ _ _

my _ _ _ _ ."

(Acts 13:22)

DAY 3
Isaiah

Just for fun

Circle the words you find. Then ignore the extra letters to find today's Scripture.

IMMANUEL. SONBWQANDDFPSHALLMG CALL
WHSAQSMVIRGINVDWSHALLBCONCEIVEBC
HEJMYYOUMJAGHQSIGN. VNBDFFHISG
FDZYLORDQHIMSELFN. VBDFBEXQANDZ
GIVEHGJWILLWBDFBEHQHISGJNAME
PLDEFBEARMBZMANDZGHEGJ
ARQVWNPKMEKNPABEFORETHEREFOREH

(Isaiah 7:14)

Discover more

Learn more about Isaiah's message in "The Voice Above" at **ClubhouseMagazine.com.**

ClubhouseMagazine.com/truth-pursuer/the-voice-above

Just for fun

Take the highlighted words from today's Scripture and put them in this puzzle. (**Hint:** Start with the word *Bethlehem* and build from there.)

But you, O **Bethlehem Ephrathah, who are too little** to be **among** the **clans of Judah**, from **you** shall **come forth for** me **one** who is to **be ruler** in **Israel, whose coming** forth **is from** of old, from **ancient days**. (**Micah** 5:2)

DAY 4
Micah

✓ **Bible fact**

What major Bible characters are linked to Bethlehem?
Bethlehem was rich in Jewish history. Rachel, Jacob's most-loved wife, was buried there, and Ruth collected barley in the fields to the east of the city. David was anointed king there. But most importantly, the Messiah was born there.

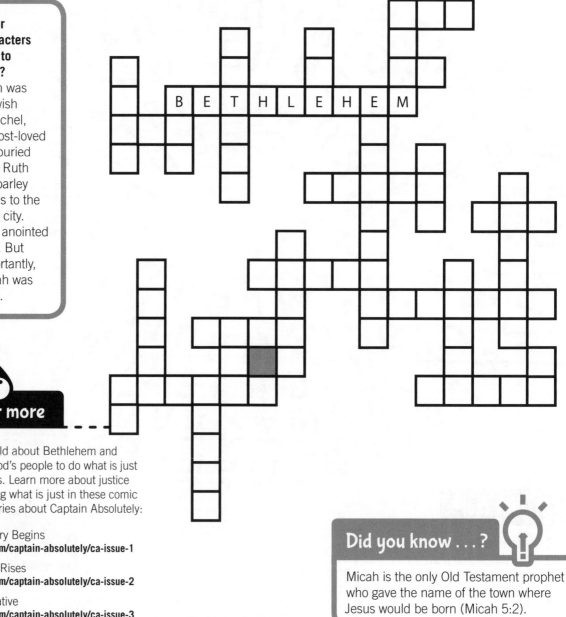

Discover more

Micah told about Bethlehem and called God's people to do what is just by others. Learn more about justice and doing what is just in these comic book stories about Captain Absolutely:

Issue No. 1: Our Story Begins
ClubhouseMagazine.com/captain-absolutely/ca-issue-1

Issue No. 2: A Hero Rises
ClubhouseMagazine.com/captain-absolutely/ca-issue-2

Issue No. 3: Dr. Relative
ClubhouseMagazine.com/captain-absolutely/ca-issue-3

Issue No. 4: Absolute Justice
ClubhouseMagazine.com/captain-absolutely/ca-issue-4

Did you know . . . ?

Micah is the only Old Testament prophet who gave the name of the town where Jesus would be born (Micah 5:2).

DAY 5
Zechariah (the prophet)

Bible fact

What did Zechariah the prophet urge people to do?
Zechariah urged people to finish rebuilding the temple and to place their hope in God.

Just for fun

The last 12 books of the Old Testament are named after the minor prophets. The men who wrote these books had a major message for Israel: Repent and turn back to God.

Fill in the rows, one letter per box, with the names of the minor prophets. **Hint:** They are *not* in the same order found in the Bible.

Hosea   Nahum
Joel   Habakkuk
Amos   Zephaniah
Obadiah   Haggai
Jonah   Zechariah
Micah   Malachi

When you've finished, read the shaded boxes to complete this sentence:

Jesus is the

_ _ _ _ _ _ _ _ _   _ _ _ _ .

Did you know . . . ?

Zechariah's name means "Yahweh remembers."

Discover more

Go deeper into the Christmas story with the short story "God's Wow Factor," found at **ClubhouseMagazine.com.**

ClubhouseMagazine.com/truth-pursuer/gods-wow-factor

Just for fun

Draw Anna's path to reach Jesus.

✓ Bible fact

How did Anna respond to seeing Jesus after He was born?
After Anna the prophetess saw Jesus, she wanted to tell others that Jesus Christ had been born.

start ←

end ←

Discover more

Did you know . . . ?

Mary and Joseph brought Jesus to the temple. A Jewish ritual required parents to bring their firstborn males to a priest. The priest would ask if the father preferred to have his son or an amount of coins, often five silver shekels. The father would give the coins to the priest, and his son would be redeemed.

The Messiah came to release humankind, who were slaves to sin. Help your child better understand slavery during Bible times by reading a story called "The Ghee" at **ClubhouseMagazine.com.**

ClubhouseMagazine.com/extras/ghee

Jesus

God the Father

FOR GOD SO LOVED THE WORLD

Isaiah

Micah

King David

Donkey

Zechariah (the prophet)

Anna

Simeon

Sheep

Zechariah (John's father)

Angel Gabriel

SAYS THE LORD

HIS NAME IS JOHN

Elizabeth

John the Baptist

King Herod

High Priest

Caesar Augustus

Innkeeper

Mary

Joseph

Angel

Wise Man on Camel

Wise Man with Gift

Wise Man with Herod

Shepherds

Heavenly Host

DAY 7
Simeon

Just for fun

Draw each square in the correct place on the grid to create your own picture of Simeon.

Did you know . . . ?

The meeting between Simeon and Jesus is celebrated by the Roman Catholic Church as *Candlemas* (also called the Presentation of the Lord) on Feb. 2.

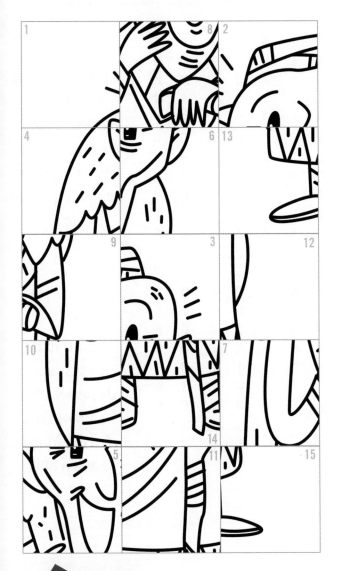

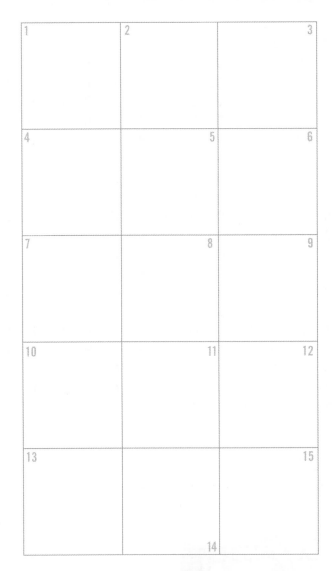

✓ **Bible fact**

Who told Simeon about Jesus?
The Holy Spirit told Simeon that he wouldn't die until he'd seen the Messiah (Luke 2:25-26).

Discover more

Read more about Simeon in "A Joyous Day" by Danika Cooley at **ClubhouseJr.com.**

www.ClubhouseJr.com/bible/joyous-day

DAY 8
Angel Gabriel

Just for fun

Search up, down, left and right for the words listed below.

Did you know . . . ?

Only two angels doing God's will are mentioned by name in the Bible: Gabriel and Michael.

```
M  I  N  E  J  A  L  T  A  R  H  A  J  I  B  A  P  H  T  I
O  A  M  S  O  N  O  H  S  E  L  A  U  C  O  L  O  M  O  N
J  O  S  P  O  G  I  S  A  L  B  F  E  N  C  A  J  O  M  Z
S  O  N  T  V  E  S  H  P  B  G  R  E  E  T  I  N  G  A  R
A  D  I  S  E  L  R  E  H  H  A  A  B  R  E  J  O  I  C  E
E  N  A  K  R  A  U  A  N  E  Z  I  H  B  O  P  L  R  O  L
L  A  H  O  S  M  N  L  A  E  S  D  E  J  U  E  K  N  N  H
I  Z  E  C  H  A  R  I  A  H  U  R  B  M  O  R  Y  A  C  R
Z  A  Z  H  A  R  I  A  X  E  S  N  E  C  N  I  E  O  E  U
A  R  R  Z  D  V  A  E  J  R  E  E  S  R  D  U  Z  Z  I  T
B  E  E  Y  O  J  A  L  A  P  H  O  T  O  B  A  T  H  V  S
E  T  N  O  W  S  H  A  N  B  U  B  A  J  F  Z  P  E  E  U
T  H  P  L  Y  A  C  H  I  N  R  N  T  H  A  O  C  I  A  O
H  V  E  L  B  I  S  S  O  P  M  I  W  E  V  H  O  C  M  E
S  H  O  U  S  A  F  A  I  N  D  G  O  T  O  R  S  T  T  T
S  A  J  W  O  O  M  B  R  D  U  R  M  A  R  Y  S  D  D  H
E  Z  U  A  S  C  J  E  P  H  A  I  B  E  M  B  R  J  O  G
H  A  T  H  E  Z  Z  U  B  S  O  V  A  E  U  I  I  E  W  I
G  L  A  D  N  E  S  S  C  E  J  M  I  R  A  Z  V  O  N  R
Z  E  R  R  S  E  B  O  R  J  O  S  E  P  H  U  J  S  E  L
```

RIDDLE

I am at the start of Gabriel, within every message and at the end of the beginning. What am I?

JOKE

Mary had Jesus, and Jesus was the Lamb of God. So did Mary have a little Lamb?

Angel	Virgin	Elizabeth	Gladness	Conceive
Zechariah	Mary	Impossible	Rejoice	Altar
Nazareth	Greeting	Righteous	Womb	Incense
	Overshadow	Afraid	Joseph	
	Joy	Favor		

Bible fact

How did people respond to the angelic visitations around the time of Jesus' birth?
Zechariah questioned Gabriel, so he lost his voice, and Mary submitted to God's will, even though she didn't wholly understand God's plan.

Discover more

Gabriel was a messenger sent to help prepare the way for Jesus' birth. Use "My Very Own Christmas Nativity" at **ClubhouseJr.com** to make your own nativity set.

ClubhouseJr.com/crafts/my-nativity

Zechariah (John's father)

Just for fun

Connect the numbered dots to draw the man God trusted to be the father of John the Baptist, who would help prepare the way for Jesus.

Bible fact

How often did a priest enter the sanctuary?
A priest may have the honor of entering the sanctuary only once or twice during his entire life.

Did you know . . . ?

Zechariah regained his voice only after the birth of his son when he wrote, "His name is John" (Luke 1:63).

HIS NAME IS JOHN

Discover more

 Zechariah needed faith to believe the angel's message from God. Learn more about faith in "Your Unchanging Friend" at **ClubhouseMagazine.com.**

ClubhouseMagazine.com/truth-pursuer/your-unchanging-friend

DAY 10
Elizabeth

✓ Bible fact

Why was Elizabeth called a "daughter of Aaron" (Luke 1:5)?
Aaron was Moses' brother. Elizabeth's family came from Aaron's priestly line. When Scripture says that she was a "daughter of Aaron," this meant that she was related to Aaron.

Did you know . . . ?

During Bible times, parents often gave their children names that were common in their family. By naming their son John, Elizabeth and Zechariah were breaking from family tradition.

Just for fun

Change one letter in each line to make another word so you can change the name "Mike" to "John."

"His name will be M I K E."

— — — —

— — — —

M O L T

— — — —

— — — —

— — — —

C O A L

— — — —

— — — —

— — — —

"His name will be J O H N."

Elizabeth was filled with joy when Mary came to visit her. Learn more about true joy by printing the board game "Christmas Joy" found at **ClubhouseJr.com.**

ClubhouseJr.com/crafts/christmas-joy

◑◑ Discover more

DAY 11
John the Baptist

Just for fun

Unscramble each word. Put the letters in the circles in order to find a word that John said a lot after he became an adult.

Bible fact

How was John set apart in his service to God?
John was set apart in his service to God from birth. He wasn't supposed to drink alcohol, and the Holy Spirit was with him even before he was born (Luke 1:15).

Did you know . . . ?

John the Baptist received this name because he baptized a lot of people as an outward sign of inward purity that came through the forgiveness of their sins.

Unscramble:

houtergi ◯ g h ◯◯ u _

misspero ◯ r _ _ i ◯ s

gnomic _ o _ _◯◯ _

John said

◯ ◯ ◯ ◯ ◯ ◯

litfafhu _ a _◯_ h _ _ l

Discover more

John told crowds of people about Jesus. Learn more about how you can tell friends about Jesus in "God in School" at **ClubhouseMagazine.com.**

ClubhouseMagazine.com/truth-pursuer/god-in-school

Learn more about John the Baptist in "River's Edge" at **ClubhouseJr.com.**

ClubhouseJr.com/bible/rivers-edge

33

✓ Bible fact

Why did Herod want the wise men to tell him where they found the newborn King?
Herod said he wanted to worship the new King, but really he wanted to kill Jesus (Matthew 2:13). Herod was the king, and he felt threatened by anyone who might become king instead of him.

Just for fun

Herod built mighty fortresses and a big, beautiful temple. He wanted to show the world what a great king he was. Today, we only remember him for his wicked heart.

Using *three* straight lines, split Herod's city into four neighborhoods. Each neighborhood must include two large houses and two small houses.
Hint: The lines don't have to go all the way across the city.

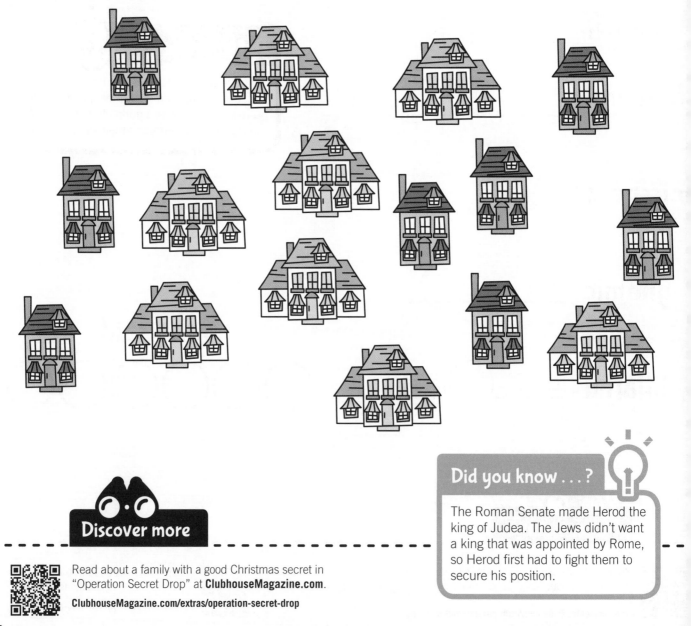

Discover more

Read about a family with a good Christmas secret in "Operation Secret Drop" at **ClubhouseMagazine.com**.

ClubhouseMagazine.com/extras/operation-secret-drop

Did you know . . . ?

The Roman Senate made Herod the king of Judea. The Jews didn't want a king that was appointed by Rome, so Herod first had to fight them to secure his position.

High Priest

Just for fun

Study these word pairs carefully. There's a letter in the first word that is missing in the second. Find the missing letters, and then fill in the blanks below to reveal Hosea 6:6.

✓ Bible fact

What were the Urim and the Thummim that only the high priest could use?
The Urim and the Thummim were special objects on or in the breastplate of the high priest's clothing. The high priest would use the Urim and the Thummim to figure out God's direction or will (Exodus 28:30).

1. _____ LAMBS ALMS

2. _____ CATTLE LATTE

3. _____ GOAT AGO

4. _____ BIRD RIB

5. _____ BLOOD BOLD

6. _____ ASHES SEAS

7. _____ FLAME MEAL

8. _____ INCENSE NICENE

9. _____ GRAIN RAIN

10. _____ FLOUR FOUR

11. _____ WINE NEW

12. _____ SHEKEL HEELS

13. _____ PRIEST TRIPS

14. _____ HANDS DASH

15. _____ WATER TEAR

16. _____ ATONE NOTE

17. _____ LEVITE ELITE

18. _____ PURE PER

19. _____ PRAYER REPAY

"
___ ___ ___   ___   ___ ___ ___ ___ ___ ___
7 5 19   11   4 13 8 11 19 13

___ ___ ___ ___ ___ ___ ___ ___ ___   ___ ___ ___ ___   ___ ___ ___
8 3 13 16 4 7 16 8 3   10 5 17 13   16 14 4

___ ___ ___   ___ ___ ___ ___ ___ ___ ___ ___ ___ , ___ ___ ___
14 5 3   8 16 2 19 11 7 11 2 13   3 6 13

___ ___ ___ ___ ___ ___ ___ ___ ___   ___ ___   ___ ___ ___
12 14 5 15 10 13 4 9 13   5 7   9 5 4

___ ___ ___ ___ ___ ___   ___ ___ ___ ___   ___ ___ ___ ___ ___
19 16 3 6 13 19   3 6 16 14   1 18 19 14 3

"
___ ___ ___ ___ ___ ___ ___ ___ ___
5 7 7 13 19 11 14 9 8   — Hosea 6:6

Discover more

Just for fun

Draw each square in the correct place on the grid to create your own picture of Caesar Augustus.

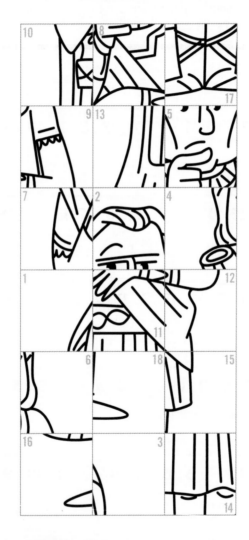

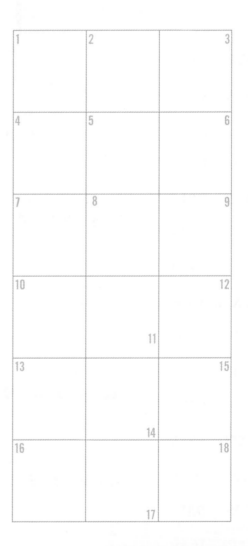

See the Bible costumes at **ClubhouseJr.com.** Then come up with your own Bible-time costume that people may have worn as they traveled for Caesar's census.

ClubhouseJr.com/crafts/bible-costumes

DAY 15
Donkey

Just for fun

Cut out the donkey and the tails. Put a piece of tape on each of the donkey tails. Blindfold the first player, turn him around a few times, have him face the wall, and then ask him to "pin" the tail on the donkey. His first touch of the wall is where the tail should be placed. His turn is over. Repeat for each player.

✓ **Bible fact**

Was it humbling to ride a donkey in Bible times?
No. People like Abraham, a patriarch, and Abigail, from a rich household, rode them. Jesus chose to ride a donkey into Jerusalem just before He died (John 12:14-15). By doing so, He fulfilled prophecy.

Did you know . . . ?

Donkeys can live for more than 50 years.

Discover more

Mary may have ridden a donkey to Bethlehem, where she gave birth to Jesus. Read about the location of Jesus' birth in "Church of the Nativity" found at **ClubhouseMagazine.com.**

ClubhouseMagazine.com/truth-pursuer/church-of-the-nativity

Use the recipe for "Double Chocolate Chip Cookies" by Christine Tangvald and Rondi DeBoer at **ClubhouseJr. com** to make your own donkey-shaped cookie. Instead of forming them by a rounded tablespoon, drop one rounded tablespoon, four legs and a head. When they bake, they will spread out, so keep them skinny when you form your donkey.

ClubhouseJr.com/recipes/double-chocolate-chip-cookies

DAY 16
Innkeeper

Just for fun

Joseph and Mary traveled from Nazareth to Bethlehem to register so Caesar Augustus would know how many people were in his kingdom. Read your way through this maze to find out what happened when they were there.

start

A	N	D	W	H	N	B	A	C	K	T	H	E	R	E	O	D	O	W	N
T	O	Y	R	I	R	Y	W	E	R	E	L	O	E	I	G	I	V	E	O
H	W	A	O	L	U	E	D	R	O	T	T	S	T	S	O	O	T	B	N
E	R	G	N	E	T	H	N	E	T	E	M	E	H	N	T	P	S	I	E
T	L	A	H	T	U	E	E	E	R	M	I	T	E	O	R	E	O	R	T
M	I	H	D	O	O	O	B	A	T	E	T	I	X	O	R	H	L	U	H
I	P	P	E	F	Y	R	T	S	R	C	A	M	E	F	O	R	Y	O	A
N	A	R	E	H	A	N	D	N	I	H	A	N	G	E	E	H	S	D	N
S	W	W	R	E	T	S	A	R	F	I	T	C	E	D	G	E	D	A	D
O	A	D	N	A	N	O	N	E	N	O	T	R	R	I	A	A	D	E	N
R	D	H	T	A	P	W	E	H	O	T	H	I	B	E	V	F	O	R	G
R	D	L	I	N	S	E	W	C	O	R	R	E	A	A	C	E	T	T	E
Y	O	L	C	G	L	E	H	N	A	E	R	C	D	L	O	G	O	H	T
E	S	O	L	C	E	R	E	I	M	G	B	T	C	P	O	I	M	E	I
B	H	T	O	O	K	H	I	M	A	N	E	C	H	S	N	N	Y	A	T
U	S	D	L	A	I	D	I	N	D	S	U	A	O	A	O	T	R	G	A
T	A	N	D	L	E	F	T	S	A	E	E	C	I	W	W	H	E	N	I
N	O	T	Q	U	I	T	E	T	E	T	H	E	R	E	A	Y	I	N	N

finish

Read a poem about the "Busy, Busy Innkeeper" at **ClubhouseJr.com**.

ClubhouseJr.com/bible/busy-busy-innkeeper

DAY 17
Sheep

Just for fun

Start -

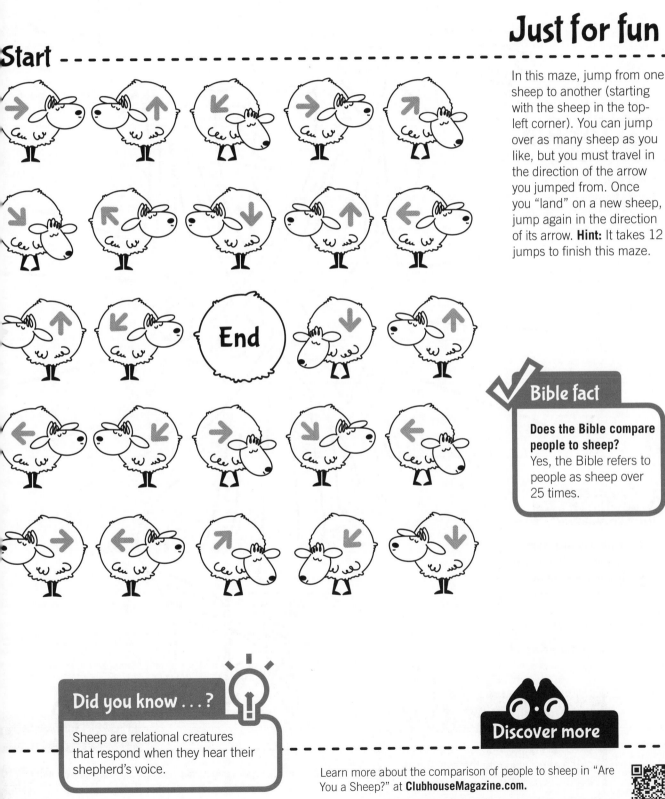

In this maze, jump from one sheep to another (starting with the sheep in the top-left corner). You can jump over as many sheep as you like, but you must travel in the direction of the arrow you jumped from. Once you "land" on a new sheep, jump again in the direction of its arrow. **Hint:** It takes 12 jumps to finish this maze.

✓ **Bible fact**

Does the Bible compare people to sheep?
Yes, the Bible refers to people as sheep over 25 times.

Did you know . . . ?

Sheep are relational creatures that respond when they hear their shepherd's voice.

Discover more

Learn more about the comparison of people to sheep in "Are You a Sheep?" at **ClubhouseMagazine.com.**

ClubhouseMagazine.com/truth-pursuer/are-you-a-sheep

DAY 18
Angel

Just for fun

- - - - - - - - - - - - - - - - -

Follow the dots to create a picture.

Did you know . . . ?

The Bible never mentions the name of the angel who told the shepherds about Jesus' birth.

Discover more

Read a short story called "Onions and Angels" at **ClubhouseMagazine.com**.

ClubhouseMagazine.com/extras/onions-and-angels

DAY 19
Shepherds

Just for fun

Use these clues to uncover a secret message. The blanks below the clues tell you how many letters are in each word.

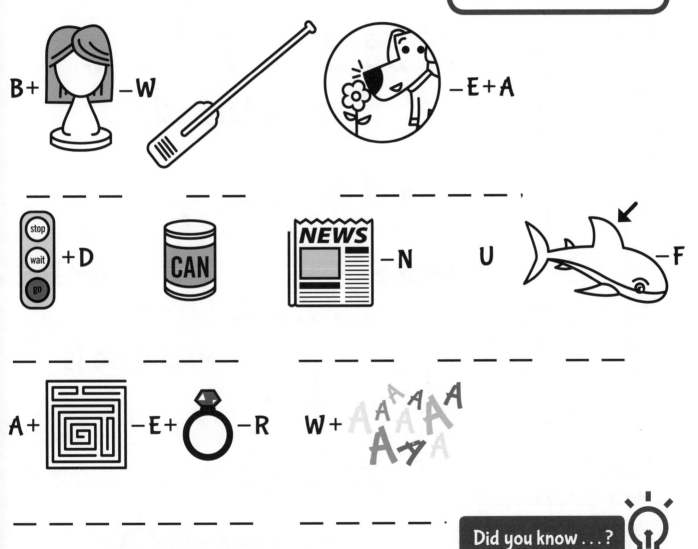

Discover more

Read this story about "A New Shepherd" at **ClubhouseJr.com**.

ClubhouseJr.com/bible/a-new-shepherd

There's more fun for you today! Act out the play, "The Interrupted Nativity," at **ClubhouseJr.com**.

ClubhouseJr.com/bible/interrupted-nativity

Bible fact

What does "heavenly host" mean?
A heavenly host refers to an army of angels.

Just for fun

Match the musical notes and symbols to the letters to form part of today's Scripture.

_____ _____ _____ _____ _____ to _____ _____ _____

in the highest,

and on _____ _____ _____ _____ _____

peace _____ _____ _____ _____ _____ those

_____ _____ _____ _____ whom he is

_____ _____ _____ _____ _____ _____ _____ !

(Luke 2:14)

Discover more

Did you know . . . ?

Angels do three things: They worship God, act as His servants and messengers, and serve in His army.

George Frideric Handel composed *Messiah*, a musical composition that people still use today to praise God, especially during the Christmas season. Many people feel the sounds of *Messiah* represent, as best as possible, how the angels may have sounded when they filled the sky with God's glory on the night of Jesus' birth. Learn the history behind this composition in "Hallelujah!" at **ClubhouseMagazine.com**.

ClubhouseMagazine.com/extras/hallelujah

Wise Men on a Journey

Who were the wise men?
The wise men were called magi, and we know that they were rich enough to bring gifts and travel a long distance. They were probably astronomers who lived east of the Roman Empire.

Just for fun

Help the magi find their way to Jesus.

start →

end ↓

Discover more

The wise men are believed to have traveled by camel from a far distance to see the new King of the Jews. Learn more about camels as a form of transportation in "Coming by Camel" at **ClubhouseJr.com.**

ClubhouseJr.com/bible/coming-by-camel

Did you know ...?

Melchior from Persia, Caspar from India and Balthazar from Arabia were written as the wise men's names in a Greek manuscript about 500 years after Jesus' birth. Because it was written a long time after the event, scholars are uncertain as to whether there is any truth to these names actually belonging to the magi.

Wise Men Talk with Herod

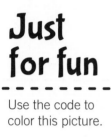

Just for fun

Use the code to color this picture.

Discover more

The wise men followed the star of Bethlehem to reach the new King, Jesus. Learn how people around the world use the image of this star to celebrate Christmas by reading "Like a Diamond in the Sky" at **ClubhouseJr.com.**

ClubhouseJr.com/bible/the-star

Bible fact

Did the wise men see Jesus when He was a baby in the manger? No. The Bible says that Jesus was in a house at the time, and Jesus is called a child, not a baby (Matthew 2:11). Herod learned about the child from the wise men. After they left, he had all the boys in Bethlehem who were two and younger killed (Matthew 2:16), probably based on the information he got from the wise men about the star's appearance.

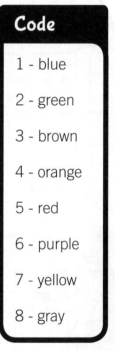

Code

1 - blue

2 - green

3 - brown

4 - orange

5 - red

6 - purple

7 - yellow

8 - gray

Did you know . . . ?

God used the wise men to help save Jesus' life. They did not tell King Herod where Jesus was in Bethlehem so the king could not kill the Messiah (Matthew 2:12).

Bible fact

How many wise men were there?
The wise men were called magi, a plural term, so we know that there were at least two of them. There were three gifts, so some assume that there were three wise men, but there could have been two wise men or many wise men. We don't know the exact number.

Just for fun

Turn these ordinary words into words from the wise men's story. Go down the column, replacing one letter at a time. Each change must result in a real word. The first column has already been done for you.

CASH	LIKE	ROAD	BALL	MEND
WASH	____	____	____	____
WISH	____	____	____	____
WISE	GIFT	STAR	GOLD	KING

Did you know . . . ?

The wise men gave Jesus gold, frankincense and myrrh. There are many theories about what each symbolized, such as gold symbolizing Jesus' earthly kingdom, frankincense honoring Him as God and myrrh symbolizing His coming death.

Discover more

Learn more about the gifts brought by the wise men in "Fit for a King" at **ClubhouseMagazine.com.**

ClubhouseMagazine.com/extras/maddie

Download a play about the journey of the three wise men in "Incredible Journey" at **ClubhouseJr.com.**

ClubhouseJr.com/bible/incredible-journey

DAY 24
Joseph

Just for fun

Search up, down, left, right, and diagonally for the names in Jesus' family tree, as written in Matthew 1. **Note:** You'll have to find "Jacob" twice.

```
M  I  N  E  J  A  B  R  L  O  H  A  J  I  B  A  P  H  T  I  M  R  E  L  U
O  A  M  S  O  L  O  H  S  E  L  I  U  S  O  L  O  M  O  N  A  B  R  O  Z
I  Z  T  B  R  S  I  S  A  L  B  R  E  N  C  A  J  O  M  Z  E  R  E  P  A
S  O  E  T  A  O  S  H  E  B  O  A  H  E  A  Z  E  K  A  R  I  A  H  A  T
A  D  I  S  H  M  R  E  T  H  A  E  B  K  J  U  R  E  H  S  H  T  A  I  A
Z  H  A  K  T  A  U  A  N  E  Z  E  H  B  O  P  L  R  E  L  A  E  D  S  H
R  E  H  O  B  M  N  L  A  E  S  S  E  J  U  E  K  A  S  H  B  P  A  A  P
E  L  I  D  U  O  A  T  K  K  U  R  B  M  O  R  Y  M  T  R  B  R  H  A  A
T  A  M  A  R  T  H  I  A  A  C  E  K  A  I  L  E  O  A  U  E  A  Y  C  H
H  D  R  Z  A  V  A  E  J  O  T  H  S  R  D  U  Z  Z  N  T  Z  O  R  T  S
M  E  E  E  N  H  A  L  A  P  H  O  T  O  B  A  T  H  S  H  E  B  A  Z  O
A  H  N  O  H  S  H  A  N  B  U  B  A  J  E  Z  N  E  T  S  A  L  M  O  H
N  A  P  L  Y  A  C  H  I  N  R  O  T  H  J  O  S  I  A  H  P  E  S  O  E
A  V  I  E  D  R  E  U  Z  Z  I  A  H  E  C  H  O  C  M  A  B  O  C  A  J
S  H  O  U  S  A  L  M  O  N  D  M  H  T  O  R  H  T  T  M  O  M  A  R  O
S  A  J  B  H  O  I  Y  R  D  U  I  M  A  B  I  U  D  H  T  A  M  A  P  T
E  Z  U  A  S  E  J  E  P  H  A  T  J  E  M  B  I  J  A  H  P  E  Z  E  H
H  A  T  H  E  Z  Z  U  B  S  O  V  A  D  U  I  L  E  T  S  A  L  O  Y  E
A  L  H  A  I  N  O  H  C  E  J  M  I  K  A  Z  R  O  N  A  D  I  R  O  J
Z  E  R  R  S  E  B  O  R  A  H  A  N  D  H  U  J  S  E  L  I  A  K  I  M
```

Abraham	Ram	Jesse	Jotham	Eliakim	Eleazar
Isaac	Amminadab	David	Ahaz	Azor	Matthan
Jacob	Nahshon	Bathsheba	Hezekiah	Zadok	Jacob
Judah	Salmon	Solomon	Manasseh	Achim	Joseph
Tamar	Rahab	Rehoboam	Amos	Eliud	Mary
Perez	Boaz	Abijah	Josiah		
Hezron	Ruth	Asaph	Jechoniah		
	Obed	Jehoshaphat	Shealtiel		
		Joram	Zerubbabel		
		Uzziah	Abiud		

Discover more

Did you know . . . ?

Jesus was born into a family—a family whose history goes all the way back to Abraham.

Bible fact

How did Mary respond when she was asked to be the mother of Jesus?
Mary had questions but gave God a place of honor in her heart. She chose to do what God wanted, even though it sounded impossible.

Just for fun

Circle the items in this list in the picture.

pencil	fish	coffee cup
rolling pin	Popsicle	basketball
scissors	candy cane	bell

Discover more

Read "This Merry Christmas Day," a Christmas poem, at **ClubhouseJr.com**.

ClubhouseJr.com/bible/merry-day

Did you know . . . ?

Joseph *and* Mary were both descendants of King David.

Just for fun

Complete the grids below so that each row, column and two-by-two box contains the letters **N-O-E-L**. (That means you can't have any repeated letters in a line or box.) When you've finished, circle the word *Noel* in each puzzle.

Did you know . . . ?

"Noel, Noel, born is the King of Israel!" *Noel* means Christmas, the day we celebrate the birth of Jesus.

Discover more

Read about the characteristics of Jesus in "What's in His Name?" at **ClubhouseMagazine.com.**

ClubhouseMagazine.com/truth-pursuer/the-name

Bible fact

How much does God love you? Watch this video to learn how much God loves you: **youtube.com/watch?v=5beoRa_HR8o.**

Kids' Puzzle Solutions

DAY 1

...ur way, O God, is holy. What god is great like our God? —Psalm 77:13

DAY 2

...ave **found** in David the son of Jesse a **man** after my **heart**, who **will** ...all my **will**." —Acts 13:22

DAY 3

...erefore the Lord himself will give you a sign. Behold, the virgin shall ...nceive and bear a son, and shall call his name Immanuel. —Isaiah 7:14

DAY 4

DAY 5

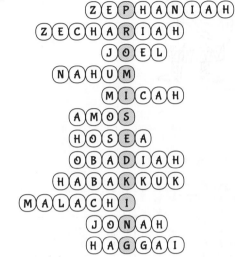

DAY 6

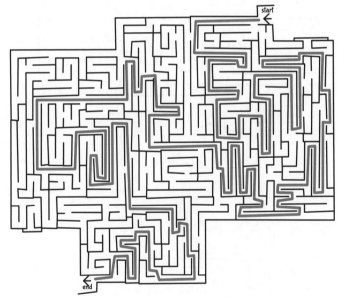

49

Solutions (continued)

DAY 7

DAY 8

I am at the start of Gabriel, within every message and at the end of the beginning. What am I?

Riddle answer: The letter G

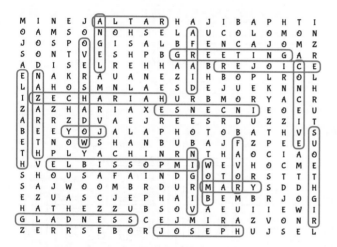

DAY 9

DAY 10

"His name will be Mike."

> Mile
> Mole
> Molt
> Moat
> Goat
> Goal
> Coal
> Coil
> Coin
> Join

"His name will be John."

DAY 11

Unscramble:	Answers:
shoutergi	**R**ighteous
misspero	**P**romises
gnomic	Coming
litfafhu	Faithful

DAY 12

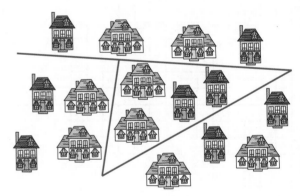

DAY 13

1. B 2. C 3. T 4. D 5. O 6. H 7. F 8. S 9. G 10. L
11. I 12. K 13. E 14. N 15. W 16. A 17. V 18. U 19. R

"For I desire steadfast love and not sacrifice, the knowledge of God rather than burnt offerings." —Hosea 6:6

50

olutions (continued)

AY 14

AY 15

the tail on the donkey

AY 16

d while they were there, the time came for her to give birth. And she
e birth to her firstborn son and wrapped him in swaddling cloths and
him in a manger, because there was no place for them in the inn.
uke 2:6-7

finish

DAY 17

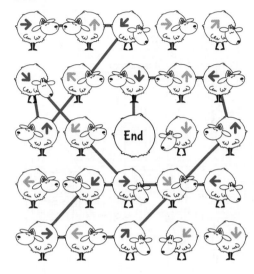

DAY 18

DAY 19

Big or small, God can use you in amazing ways.

DAY 20

"**Glory** to **God** in the highest, and on **earth** peace **among** those **with**
whom he is **pleased**!" —Luke 2:14

Solutions (continued)

DAY 21

DAY 24

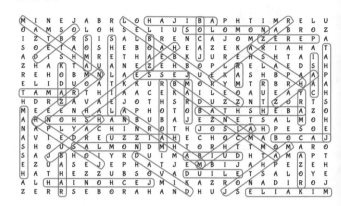

DAY 25

DAY 22

DAY 23

CASH	LIKE	ROAD	BALL	MEND
WASH	LIFE	ROAR	BALD	MIND
WISH	LIFT	SOAR	BOLD	KIND
WISE	GIFT	STAR	GOLD	KING

CHRISTMAS DAY CELEBRATION

E	L	O	N
O	N	L	E
N	O	E	L
L	E	N	O

N	L	O	E
E	O	L	N
L	N	E	O
O	E	N	L

O	L	N	E
N	E	O	L
L	O	E	N
E	N	L	O